ROCK & SAND

A Practical Insight to Business Growth

BY MICHAEL SYNK

WITH THE GRAVITAS COMMUNITY

www.rocknsand.net

In-Synk: Aligning Strategy, Actions and Goals
1599 Vinton Avenue
Memphis, TN 38104

www.in-synk.com

Cover Design and Layout by Tactical Magic

ISBN: 9781090496386

TESTIMONIALS

"Effective business leaders must know the answers to two fundamental questions that drive profitable growth: "What is our strategy?" and "How will we make that happen?" Both are regularly overcomplicated beyond practicality by authors, experts, and consultants with a stake in promoting strategy as a complicated enterprise. Michael Synk has created a straightforward, simple model that not only debunks the complexity myth, but also facilitates execution - getting things done - as an integral component of good strategy. If you're serious about growing your business and if you're a fan of simplicity over complexity - this is the book for you."

—Mark Green, President, Performance Dynamics Group LLC

"Have you ever wondered about the analogy of moving 'rocks' used by many strategy advisers? I have always found it a peculiar analog. Where are we moving them? I imagined my team lugging big rocks down a field on a hot day and measuring success as an end zone. Michael's explanation and visualization is something that fits the world view of my team and me. As a team we push sand and can always do that bigger, faster, or stronger. We all know that's not strategic but easy to point to as progress. Strategic growth occurs when my team gets behind a big rock and we push hard and collectively to fill in big gaping holes in our business. It is the sustainable foundation of both rocks and sand on which all businesses need to stand."

—Eric Mathews, Founder and CEO Start Co,
a venture development organization and startup ecosystem
builder in the Southeastern United States.

CONTENTS

FOREWORD

"We are the smartest person in the room…" These words still echo in my ears from senior business coach Ted (Ernst) Sarvata, while leading a planning session way back in 2010. What does this phrase mean in practicality? It means "The combined intellect, effort and experience of a trusting community can solve almost any challenge or opportunity presented to them."

Thus, behind this simple concept, the foundation of this Premium Edition of Rock & Sand came to be under the vision and leadership of original author Michael Synk. Michael had penned the original in 2013, and it quickly grew in interest, impact, and use worldwide, primarily due to the simplicity, ease of use, and proven nature of the content and tools it shared and advocated.

In the Spring of 2018, our worldwide coaching community of 250 business coaches experienced an unexpected trauma to the organization that resulted in pain, confusion and distraction for all involved. As the community worked through the process of recovery, stabilization, and a return to growth, the noble character of many individual coaches came shining through, out of a love for our trusting community, its core values and its purpose. Michael Synk was one of the first leaders in our community to stand up and challenge our peers to use our misfortune for "The Good of the Order" (one of our Core Values) by tapping into the intellect, experience, and effort of the community to take "Rock & Sand" to a deeper, more robust level of value for business owners, non-profit executive directors, and community leaders.

Michael and the contributing members of our coaching community felt our clients and the larger business community needed a simple set of proven principles and tools to organize, focus and grow their organizations. Michael organized about a dozen volunteer coaches worldwide to rewrite this Premium Edition of Rock & Sand as a community, a term we refer to in our circles as "Coach Sourced."

If you are student of business, and drill down on the principles and research underneath each concept and chapter in Rock & Sand, you will see the fingerprints and footprints of Jim Collins, Michael Porter, Jack Stack, Bob Bloom, Verne Harnish, Pat Lencioni and others (to name a few, but not all of the contributory Thought Leaders) - and we wish to acknowledge and extend our gratitude to them all.

The beauty of Rock & Sand is not only in its simple and timeless principles, but also the eloquent and insightful pen of each chapter's author, forged with decades of experience helping mid-market companies and nonprofits grow, scale, and succeed.

A "tip of the hat" not only to Michael for his vision and leadership, but also to those who have come before us all in our legacy of coaching DNA: Dan Weston (Emeritus Coach); Ron Huntington (Emeritus Coach); and a man most of us have never heard of, Don Lusk, who started it all, without really knowing it, by taking the time to mentor one young, character-driven, impressionable yet enthusiastic coach. Thank you, Don. Your legacy lives on in this work from Michael Synk and our greater "Coach Sourced" Community.

— Keith Cupp, Coach & CEO Gravitas Impact Premium Coaches
February 2019

PART ONE – THE ROCK & SAND MODEL
STRATEGY IS EVERYWHERE

Strategy comes in all shapes and sizes to fit all sorts of organizations, from enormous to tiny. It fits all markets, segments, industries, personalities, income levels, nations, states, counties, cities and neighborhoods.

Of course, books about strategy abound. A simple search in March of 2013 of "Business Strategy " on amazon.com brings up a list of over 40,000 titles. As you read this, rest assured there is at least one more added to the list each month. You've heard the litany of titles: *Blue Ocean Strategy; Big Think Strategy; Good Strategy, Bad Strategy; Strategic DNA; Strategic Planning for Dummies, The Lords of Strategy, The Art of Strategy, Thinking Strategically, The Strategist, The Strategy Focused Organization*....and so on. Multiple books on strategy have been written by Porter, Peters, Hamel, Pralahad, Collins, Deming, and Drucker. Every professor of strategy trying to achieve tenure has written one as well. Don't forget that the titans of business have to write them too. Jack Welch has written three and there is one from every one of his lieutenants who left the fold to make a fortune elsewhere. The genre has been around a long time starting with Sun Tzu's *The Art of War*.

Are you getting the picture? There isn't a lack of guidance about strategy.

I've read many of these books, and I've put much of what I've learned from them to work with my clients. There are lots of ways to develop good strategy. Having different ways to look at strategy can be enlightening, stimulating the creative thought that creates the best plans.

Yet within this vast library of books on strategy, something is missing. Concrete models for execution are largely absent from the material. Execution is almost entirely left up to the reader.

Don't think that "Business Execution" books don't exist either. amazon.com lists over 5000, a much smaller number. I've read a number of these books as well, and most are worthwhile. But, of the ones I've read, none of them tie execution back to strategy.

This is a gross oversimplification, but all the execution literature seems to be progressions of the priority and time management principles outlined originally by Ben Franklin in his "Autobiography," only expanded to fit teams and organizations. They articulate important leadership tactics for getting things done faster, better, and with less energy. Yet, like the strategy books, tying these important habits back to strategy is left up to the reader.

This "missing link" between strategy and execution is a problem. Good strategies are developed but don't get executed. Great execution habits are learned and applied to actions that lead organizations to places they don't want to go. Very quickly strategy and execution turn into doing what was already being done, only now with an emphasis on faster, better, and harder.

This type of strategy and execution is one dimensional. "More is better, let's do more." It's rigid, it's tedious, it's expensive. Growth can be steady, yet it is hardly exponential. When significant growth occurs, it is a function of serendipity, not intent. It's strategy after the fact, backfilled from results.

Yet this is where the vast majority of businesses live, strategically and execution-wise.

We need a way to think and speak about strategy and execution that is simple, productive, and definitive that builds a bridge between strategy and execution. It needs it to be fundamentally sound and motivationally inspiring, so that strategy and execution is aligned and linked.

We don't need another strategy or execution book. We need a book that spans the gap between the two. That's what this book is about.

As with most things worth thinking, talking, and writing about, it often comes down to asking the right question. Here it is.

Are you "pushing sand" or "moving rocks"?

PART ONE – THE ROCK & SAND MODEL

ARE YOU "PUSHING SAND" OR "MOVING ROCKS"?

You're "pushing sand" when you are performing the basic tasks of your business. A comprehensive list of these activities includes the following: advertising, sales, taking orders, making product, delivering service, billing, and collecting. In short, these are the activities that must be done to transact business. Do them poorly, the sand slips between your fingers, and you lose money. Do them well and you make money. "Pushing sand" is pretty basic concept. You have to do it well to stay in business.

You're "moving rocks" when you are working on something that makes "pushing the sand" easier, faster, or more profitable. When "moving a rock," you might be adding a product line, or you might be improving a production process. You could be expanding your territory, or you could be expanding your technology. It could be a new sales campaign, a new marketing campaign, or a new safety campaign. It could be as simple as adding one especially well qualified employee, or as complicated as adding a whole new department. Sometimes it's not about adding but subtracting: narrowing your focus, narrowing your offerings, or eliminating steps and waste. But whatever the rock, moving it makes it easier to push more sand faster and for more profits.

Here's how you know the difference between rocks and sand. There are three possible situations:

1. You are pushing sand, but not moving rocks. If you are successful at pushing the sand, you are surviving but only until someone figures out how to do it better than you. You aren't really growing.

2. You are moving rocks, but not pushing sand. You are still proving your business model. You don't have cash flow. You've got to find and push some

sand before you can say you are growing.

3. You are pushing sand successfully and moving rocks productively. You are finding ways to push more and more sand. Your business is quite likely growing.

Which of the three situations is best for your company?

PART ONE – THE ROCK & SAND MODEL
THE ROCK AND SAND MODEL

Let's visualize this model.

Imagine that the current status of your company is the bottom of a deep hole, something like a mineshaft or well and you are working your way up from. Where you want to be in three to five years is your long-term goal. You want to get from where you are right now to where you will be the future. This is what it looks like.

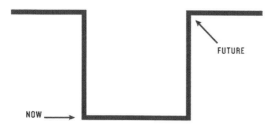

On one side of the hole there is a pile of sand: a big pile of sand, which represents the basic tasks of your company that are done to transact business. Completing these activities equates to pushing sand into the hole. The more you complete the more sand you are pushing into the hole. The sand piles up in the hole and your company gets a bit closer to the top of the whole. It looks something like this:

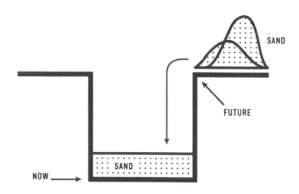

Pushing sand takes a lot of time and effort. It's tedious at the least and exhaustive at its worst. It moves your company rather slowly towards the top of the hole. To push greater amounts of sand into the hole requires equal increases in both time and effort. The return on effort is low.

On the other side of the hole is a pile of big rocks. Each one represents a different new initiative that if completed could make it easier for you to push more sand or get more value for the sand you are already pushing. When you complete one of these initiatives, you are moving a rock into the hole. It takes up space and allows the sand to pile up faster, moving your company to the top of the hole faster than before. It looks like this:

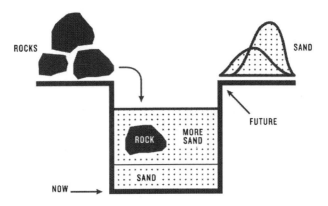

Over time, you keep pushing sand and moving rocks; pushing sand to transact business and moving rocks so you can transact business more easily, faster and for a bigger return. When done successfully, you reach your goal more quickly, in effect getting to the top of the hole faster.

PART ONE – THE ROCK & SAND MODEL
NO ROCKS, NO GROWTH

It comes down to this: if your company isn't moving rocks, it isn't growing.

Think about it in terms of our analogy. While sand may be easy to work with, it's hardly a foundation for growth. Sand is almost fluid, isn't it? It shifts with the wind. It melts into mud with the addition of water. It can dissipate instantaneously.

The sand your enterprise is pushing into its hole can change just as quickly. Markets change, competitors appear, technologies evolve, the economy shifts. Your sand pile can literally disappear overnight.

Rocks, on the other hand, are more formidable. They take up space. They have size and weight. They can fit together and have a multiplier effect on each other. They have substance. Moving them, albeit difficult, makes a difference and changes the lay of the land.

Moving rocks changes the landscape as well, only this time to your benefit. Consider the following rocks:

- A new product line helps you to push more sand without adding new customers. Or maybe it adds a whole new set of customers.

- New talent brought into the company helps you see better ways to push the sand.

- A technology upgrade can make the pushing of sand more efficient.

- Fresh market research helps you find more piles of sand from new markets that you can push.

- A new or improved process lets you deploy resources to other opportunities.

In each case the trajectory of the business changes.

If you aren't working on a rock your business is at best standing still and at worst moving backward. Even if your sand pile is big and your results look good on paper, your business is not growing. The results are illusory and will disappear as the sand pile shifts, gets blown away, or just plain runs out.

You have to move rocks to achieve sustainable growth.

PART ONE – THE ROCK & SAND MODEL
WHICH ROCK IS THE RIGHT ONE?

So which rock do you push?

It's a difficult question.

There are a lot of potential rocks to move and with so many to choose from, the decision to focus on just one can be paralyzing in and of itself. Here are some rules for figuring this out.

<u>Never, ever, try to move more than one or two rocks at one time.</u> Trying to move more dilutes your efforts and resources. Let's say you have determined that you have five rocks you think you need to move this year. And, as I have often witnessed, you enlist a team to take responsibility for each one. Remember that these teams are full of individuals who are also working hard to push sand, which is their primary responsibility. Each rock gets moved a little bit, but not all the way into the hole, resulting in incremental improvements in a number of areas, but no real impact that makes a significant difference and delivers growth. Instead, limit yourself to one rock, or at most two, and align the entire team around moving the rock. More people giving more effort in a concentrated and collaborative manner gets the job done.

<u>Don't select a "me too," rock.</u> By this I mean don't pick a rock just because a competitor or other companies are working on something similar. Following the herd is rarely a good move. Make sure there are other reasons for your selection, reasons that are truly relevant to your situation. Don't be lured by the shiny rocks that exist, either, and avoid trendiness. Select a few of these "me too" rocks in a row and you will wear your team out without much result.

<u>Think about the rock that will have the biggest impact or make the biggest difference.</u> What's the biggest problem to be solved or the biggest opportunity to capitalize on? Is there a rock you can move that significantly closes the gap on a

problem or eliminates it? Is there a rock you can move that will help you exploit the opportunity faster or better or more profitably? Is there a rock you can move that changes the game entirely? Think through these questions thoroughly and determine which rock in your pile fits this one of these scenarios. Quantify and qualify and make a selection. And then set it aside for a moment to address the dilemma outlined in the next paragraph.

<u>Does another rock come first?</u> Often you and your team aren't ready to move the biggest and most important rock. Something else comes first. Maybe you don't have the talent, maybe you don't have the knowledge, or the cash, or the technology. Maybe you have to learn how to work together first. Maybe something has to be put in place or removed to be able to get to the rock. Maybe the big all-important rock is too big to move right now and you have to move a few to be ready to move the important one.

<u>What does the calendar look like?</u> This last question is helpful to work through when determining time frames for each rock. Some rocks are best moved during certain times of the year as opposed to others. Maybe you have a busy season, where the rock for that particular period can't be anything else except "getting through the busy season" as productively as possible. Maybe there is a special event or two or three on your calendar, such as important tradeshows or conferences that can't be ignored and must be worked through.

Think through and argue through each one of these rules, then select a rock and commit to it.

PART ONE – THE ROCK & SAND MODEL
THE BIG SIX STRATEGY QUESTIONS

The previous section outlines a process for determining which rock is the right one. It works pretty well. But if you start the process after answering the Big Five Strategy Questions, it works even better.

Consider these Big Six Strategy Questions?

1. <u>Why do we exist?</u> – The answer to this question gives your company both meaning and purpose. It is often referred to by strategy experts as the Purpose Statement or Mission Statement. It should be simple and clear. It expresses what is at the heart of the business. It adds noble purpose and aspiration to the enterprise.

2. <u>How should we behave?</u> – The answers to these questions are the DNA of the company. They convey to the team what is and isn't desired behavior. Strategy experts refer to these as Core Values. They go beyond simple "permission to play" values such as honesty and integrity. They express the spirit of team, the tone of behavior, and the ethical pillars of the company.

3. <u>What are we good at?</u> – Often referred to as Core Competencies, these answers tell you where to begin and build on. These are the processes and procedures you are best at, or can get better at than anyone else in your market or industry. It's the starting point of strategy; it's the strengths of your company that you build or add to in order to grow.

4. <u>Where do we want to end up?</u> – Every company needs a sense of direction in order to grow. This is the long term outcome for the company. It's often referred to as the Vision. Jim Collins calls it the Big Hairy Audacious Goal (BHAG). It's where you are going and where you want to end up at least ten years down the road.

5. <u>Who is our Core Customer?</u> – Going beyond the demographics of the customer that we have all been trained to identify, is your "Who" clear. By "Who" I mean the "person" who is buying from you: what are his/her traits, behaviors, workload, education, challenges both at work and at home, going way beyond the immediate problem or challenge your product or company solves.

6. <u>Why should customers do business with us?</u> – Is there a compelling reason for customers to buy from you or use your service? It usually isn't price. It needs to be customer-driven not company-driven. It addresses the needs of your key customers and expands from there to other customer groups. It is often referred to as the Brand Promise, or Value Proposition.

When you answer these questions, write them down, and use them by actively and regularly sharing them with your team. Your Big Six Answers become guardrails for all of the decisions about growth for your team, keeping the company moving down the highway and out of the ditches that line the road. Most importantly they create the context for the process of selecting the right rock. Context is king when selecting a rock.

There are lots of ways determine and codify the answers to these questions. Having been a Gravitas Premium Impact Coach for more than 15 years, I recommend using the **Baseline Growth Roadmap**™ and the **Four Decisions**™ **Model** developed by Gravitas. They match up perfectly with the **Rock & Sand Model**™ outlined in this book (there is a download link to the Gravitas Tools in the implementation section of this book). Other methodologies work well too. It's not about the form or format. It's about facilitating deep dialogue within your company, supported by data that uncovers the answers to the Big Six Strategy Questions.

PART ONE – THE ROCK & SAND MODEL

DO THE NUMBERS: THREE YEARS, ONE YEAR, NEXT 90 DAYS

After determining your Big Six Strategy Answers, it's time to look forward and predict the future for your business. Set some specific outcomes for your business, some milestones to hit somewhere down the road.

Use your Big Six Strategy Answers to guide you in a game of "Let's Pretend." Pick a year three years out and pretend that you have been relatively successful at living out the Big Six Strategy Answers. Envision your team is living the Core Values, your team is building their Core Competencies and leveraging them to deliver your Brand Promise to your Core Customers. Extrapolate from this scenario and conceptualize the positive results your company has achieved. Pretend that all of it is happening because the team is sticking to the Purpose or Mission of the company. And finally, pretend you have moved closer to reaching your BHAG.

Extend the game of "Let's Pretend" and predict what numbers you have hit three years out: Revenue, expenses, net profit, cash flow, market share, number of customers, revenue per employee. Do the same for any industry-specific numbers you measure or track.

Work backwards from your three year projection and decide what numbers you have to hit in the coming year to be able to hit your three year numbers.

Work backwards from one year and set the numbers you have to hit in the next 90 days to be able to hit your one year numbers.

Play this game of "Let's Pretend" in pencil. Keep playing with the numbers until you are comfortable with them. They should be realistic, but also ambitious. They might be difficult to achieve if all you do is continue to push the sand, but easier to accomplish if you figure out the right rocks to move that makes them attainable.

PART ONE – THE ROCK & SAND MODEL
THRUSTS –> INITIATIVES –> ROCKS

The game of "Let's Pretend" continues.

Once again you'll be working backwards from three years to one year to the next 90 days.

Knowing and accepting the numbers that you need to hit for three years, ask and then answer the following questions:

1. What capabilities or competencies are missing that we need to have in place in next three years to hit the three year projections?

2. What do we have to get better at or learn in the next three years to hit the numbers?

3. What departments/technologies/people do we need to add in the next three years to hit the numbers?

The answers to these questions will be the key thrusts of your company for the next three years. Don't worry too much about how you will execute them right now. Just decide on them and commit to them.

Continue the game with the one year time frame. Knowing that you have to hit the one year numbers and that to hit the three year numbers you have to make progress on the Key Thrusts, ask and then answer this question:

Breaking down the key thrusts into parts, what three to five rocks should I move this year that will move the company forward?

When answering this question keep two things in mind. First, while you are moving these rocks during the next year, the team has to keep pushing sand, so don't bite off more than you can chew. Second, be cognizant of the resources you have available to assign to these rocks. An additional rock might be shifting people or adding a person to be able move one of the rocks. This might become a rock in and of itself.

The rocks you decide to move on, in the coming year, are your initiatives.

Finally, extend the game to the next 90 days. There is only one question to answer at this point.

Which one or two of these rocks should we move right now? (review section 5)

Again, keep in mind that in the next 90 days, while you are moving the rock you select, your company has to continue pushing sand.

PART ONE – THE ROCK & SAND MODEL
THE LITTLE THREE EXECUTION QUESTIONS

Now that you have identified your it's time to apply the *Little Three Execution Questions*.

WHO? WHAT? WHEN?

From a big picture point of view you have already answered two of the questions: "What" is the rock and the "When" is 90 days from now. The "Who" is the person who is responsible for making sure the rock gets moved successfully. Responsibility has to be assigned to one and only one person. Others can be assigned to the team that moves the rock and can be assigned accountability for certain parts of the rock, but only one person can be responsible. When multiple people are responsible for one thing, no one is responsible.

You aren't done with the Little Three Execution Questions yet. The "Who" that has taken responsible for the rock needs to take "Who, What, and When" to the entire team he will be working with to move the rock. The team should create a to do list on all the items that need to be completed in the process of moving the rock, then for each particular task the leader needs to ask "What will be done?" "Who will do it?" and "When it will be completed?"

At least weekly, review this "Who, What, When" list. Check off what is accomplished; figure out how to check off the ones that are stalled. List new items to be added to the list as you move forward, adding the "Who" and the "When" until your list is complete. Keep this rhythm going until your the rock is completely moved into the hole.

The Little Three Execution Questions just might be more powerful than the Big Six Strategy Questions. They are about getting things done. They keep commitments front and center and help you measure progress. They keep the team engaged and moving forward, which in turn moves your company forward.

Shouldn't you be using "Who, What, When" on every actionable item in your company?

PART ONE – THE ROCK & SAND MODEL
WHAT ABOUT THE SAND?

Don't ever forget about the sand.

When everyone is excited and working hard at moving a rock, it's easy to forget about the sand. Don't ever let this happen. If you do, you are putting your company at risk. You'll run out of the cash you need to move the rocks. Rocks don't fund you, the sand does. Pushing sand creates the revenue and then the profits that become the cash that pays for the resources needed to move your rock. If you don't keep pushing the sand, you won't be moving any rocks for very much longer. Your business will shrink instead of growing.

It's not a case of choosing to move the rock or to push the sand. You have choose to move the rock and push the sand at the same time.

While choosing your rock for the quarter, and committing the proper resources to moving it, the same attention must be applied to the sand. Give the sand equal status to the rock. Commit to pushing it and commit succeeding at it. Use the Little Three Execution Questions to do this.

- Assign responsibility and accountability for each part of pushing the sand. (Who)

- Determine the activities that push the sand and measure them. (What)

- Set some milestones to hit (When)

- Review the sand at the weekly same weekly meetings where you review progress on the rock. This keeps the sand and their milestones front of mind for the entire company.

It's perfectly fine for a small part of the team to focus on moving the current rock while the rest of the team stays focused on pushing the sand. In this scenario, a few are entirely devoted to the rock, while the rest contribute to the rock by pushing the sand. Keep both groups informed on the progress of the other.

Another way to do this is to have everyone take part in moving the rock while at the same time continuing to push the sand.

Either way works. Picking one way or the other is related to the particular rock you are moving, the talent on your team, and configuration of your company. Mixing it up each quarter works also works well.

But whatever you do, don't stop pushing the sand.

PART ONE – THE ROCK & SAND MODEL
PICK A ROCK, MOVE IT, REPEAT

This brings us back to the beginning doesn't it? Let's review.

No matter what, your company has to keep pushing the sand, pushing more of it, and doing it better. But your company has to move rocks, while at the same time pushing the sand, or your company won't grow. And you can't move just any rocks. You have to move the right ones so that they build on each other and take your company where you want it to go.

To insure that you have selected the right rocks, you must first answer the Big Six Strategy Questions. This creates context for your selections. Then you set milestones to meet three years out, one year out and for the next 90 days. At this point identify key thrusts, narrow them down to three to five rocks to move in the coming year and then select the right rock for the next 90 days.

Finally, you ask the Little Three Execution questions to make sure you move the rock.

Pick a rock. Move it. Repeat. Pick another rock. Move it. Repeat.

All the while, simultaneously pushing the sand.

At the most basic level, this is what strategy and execution is all about.

Good Luck.

PART TWO – IMPLEMENTING THE ROCK & SAND MODEL
GRAVITAS IMPLEMENTATION TOOLS

www.gravitasimpact.com/rockandsand

I realize I made a mistake with the original edition of Rock & Sand. In my effort to simplify your understanding of strategy and execution, and the connection between the two, I only made reference to what the elements of a good strategic plan was. I didn't exactly reveal how you create or identify them or how to use it effectively to unleash growth from your company. I believe I've corrected that in this edition.

I've gone to the Gravitas Impact Premium Coaches' toolbox and pulled out the tools that we use to help our clients create these elements when working with them. There are thirteen of them and you can download them at this link. **www.gravitasimpact.com/rockandsand**

Additionally, I've asked nine of my peers in Gravitas to write instructional chapters on how to use each of the tools. Each coach, with contact information, is listed at the top of the chapter they authored so you can contact them if you have questions.

Each of the tools represents, not a task to be done, but a thought process to go through to create each of the elements needed to build a good plan that will unleash your company's growth. As you proceed through the following chapters, you will learn that strategy is a team sport, not an individual one. The thought process of each tool requires deep dialogue among the people who you will rely on to execute the plan. As the leader of the organization, your most important function is to use each tool to create the meaningful dialogue, listen to it, then get it right, and then add the outcomes of all the tools together to create a great strategic plan.

Good strategy is rarely created by the person at the top and handed down to the minions. Very few have the genius of Steve Jobs, he was one of a kind. The best leaders, the real geniuses, are genius makers. They create the dialogue that gets everyone thinking more strategically and engages them to make a better strategy than they could have created on their own.

By following the instructions outlined in the remaining chapter, you'll be creating alignment among the future geniuses of your company. And that, ultimately, is what unleashes the growth.

PART TWO – IMPLEMENTING THE ROCK & SAND MODEL
THE BASELINE GROWTH ROADMAP™

By Michael Synk | **www.in-synk.com**

There is a saying we use at Gravitas, that many other strategy coaches use as well. "If you can't get it down on one piece of paper, it's probably too complicated."

Here's a few other versions of the end of that saying.

"…. no one will be able to understand it"

"…. you won't be able to execute it"

"…. it will be impossible to share with others."

''…. you'll forget about what's most important."

"…. it will probably be put on a shelf."

The Baseline Growth Roadmap™ addresses the various versions of this saying. It's a one-page repository of the all the elements of your strategic plan, it keeps things simple; it makes the plan easy to explain to others; it creates accountability for execution; it allows for sharing; it keeps the current rocks front and center and top of mind; and it can easily be pulled out to guide you on decisions and track progress.

It will keep everyone aligned, informed, and making the good decisions that unleash growth.

As you go through the planning process, make sure everyone has copy of it in front of them. As you complete each portion of it, have everyone pencil in what was decided into the corresponding section, and have one person keep a master copy on their computer. When each person writes down what is completed, as it is completed, they learn it better, become more committed to it, and develop a sense of accomplishment as the plan builds. When fully completed, they can get to work immediately on the parts of the play they impact.

Using the rest of the Gravitas Tools to guide the dialogue, complete each section one by one. Keep in mind though, that creating a strategic plan is not necessarily a linear process. It's more like a crossword puzzle. Feel free to jump around when filling it in, especially if you feel you have parts of it already identified.

Don't worry about perfect, that's for later. Gut it out. Get it down. Get going with it. Make it perfect later. It's a Baseline Growth Roadmap. It's meant to get the basics of your strategy down so you can start executing it.

It's also an evolving plan. Remember you will come back to it, update it, test it, adjust it, each quarter.

ROCK —&— SAND | BASELINE Growth Roadmap™

FOUNDATION		3 YEARS
CORE	**STRATEGY**	**TARGETS**

Core Purpose

BHAG®

3HAG™

Year	
Revenue	
Gross Profit	
Cash	
%Adjust 1	
%Adjust 2	
%Adjust 3	

Core Values

Profit Per X

Core Customer

Key Thrusts

1

2

3

Core Strengths

Brand Promise

3HAG™ Critical Numbers

• _____

• _____

• _____

Organization:

Name: Date:

ROCK & SAND   G

1 YEAR	90 DAYS

GOALS	ACTIONS	PERSONAL PLAN

1HAG

Year	
Revenue	
Gross Profit	
Cash	
Widget 1	
Widget 2	
Widget 3	

90-Day Plan

Quarter	
Revenue	
Gross Profit	
Cash	
Widget 1	
Widget 2	
Widget 3	

Personal Critical Number

1

2

3

4

Annual Priorities

1

2

3

Quarterly Priorities   Who

1

2

3

Personal Priorities

1

2

3

1HAG Critical Numbers

•

•

•

Critical Numbers

•

•

•

Personal Development

•

•

•

PART TWO – IMPLEMENTING THE ROCK & SAND MODEL
CORE PURPOSE

By Chris Kenny | **www.stargroupconsulting.com**

One of the best ways to uncover your company's Core Purpose is follow the team-based process developed by Jim Collins and Jerry Porras called the "Five Whys." This process is documented in the Gravitas Core Purpose Tool you downloaded earlier.

Setup: Gather your executive team together and ask them to help you make sure the organization is aligning all its key decisions with its Core Purpose, that you want everyone to understand it, and that they use the Core Purpose as they make all future decisions.

On one wall, hang two self-stick flip chart sheets. One should be labeled, "Descriptive Statement," and the other should be labeled, "Core Purpose." Give everyone a copy of the Gravitas Core Purpose Tool.

Step 1: On the flip chart labeled, "Descriptive Statement," write a brief description of the product or service your company sells. For example, "We manufacture circuit boards for personal computers" or "We deliver training classes to human resource professionals." Discuss this briefly to ensure consensus among the team members that you have an accurate description of your product or service.

Step 2: Work through the "Five Whys" using the Gravitas Core Purpose Tool. While working through the tool, participants should work by themselves and not share their answers until Step 3. Allow three to five minutes for each "Why" on the tool.

1. Looking at the Descriptive Statement, and taking into account our shareholders/owners, employees, suppliers, customers and our community, why do you believe that Descriptive Statement is important?

2. When you have answered that ask another "Why." "Why does that answer you wrote for Question 1 matter?" Again, no one reads their answers.

3. When finished ask another "Why" "Why is the answer you wrote for Question 2 important?" Again, they document their answers without sharing them.

4. When finished with that answer ask another "Why" "Why does the answer you wrote for Question 3 matter?" Again, they document their answers without sharing.

5. Finally, when everyone is finished with the last question ask "Why" one more time. "Why." "Why is the answer you wrote for Question 4 important?" They once again document their answers without sharing them.

Step 3: After everyone completes the "Five Whys," go around the room and ask each individual to read their answers to just Question 1 and Question 5, without explaining them, and post them on the flip chart named Core Purpose. After everyone has done this, allow for clarifying questions to ensure that everyone clearly understands what each person has said. Now take 10 – 15 minutes to dialogue on the responses as a group to settle on an answer to the fifth "Why" that feels most "correct" for the organization. Cross out the answers that don't apply. Re-write the remaining answers to clear up language if needed and document it the Baseline Growth Roadmap.

Even if your Core Purpose statement doesn't feel "perfect" right now, recognize that it is mostly right and start using it. In the future you can work to improve it. Then make sure the Core Purpose is communicated throughout the organization, that it is referred to in team meetings, and referenced when making key decisions. When your team hears it being said regularly and sees it being used constantly everyone will "buy in" to what the organization is really all about.

ROCK & SAND

Core Purpose: Your Company's Reason for Being

FOUR DECISIONS® Tools

Attributes of a company's Core Purpose:

- Higher purpose (beyond profit and jobs)
- Does not change…but inspires change
- Engages team members emotionally
- Causes team to work around/through obstacles

Descriptive Statement

"What does your company do today"

1. **WHY** is it important?

2. **WHY** does this matter?

3. **WHY** is it important?

4. **WHY** does this matter?

5. **WHY** is it important?

OUR CORE PURPOSE

Note: What was the founder's original passion or purpose in starting the company?

Four Types of Core Purpose:

- Service to others
- Search for knowledge and truth
- Pursuit of beauty and excellence
- Desire to change the world

PART TWO – IMPLEMENTING THE ROCK & SAND MODEL
CORE VALUES

By Kirsti Tcherkoyan | **www.options4growth.com**

Use the Mission to Mars exercise to determine your core values and to promote a positive culture. Use the Core Values Tool to complete the Mission to Mars exercise.

Give everyone on the team a copy of the tool. Each team member fills it out individually, writing down the names and corresponding admirable attributes of employees who model great values.

After everyone has finished, ask each person to write the attributes they have noted, on sticky notes and post all of them on a large wall. Once all the notes are posted, the whole team is invited to stand up and group similar attributes together, completely in silence.

Once the notes have been grouped together, take a step back.

Together as a team, go through each grouping and dialogue deeply about what stands out and why. Your goal is to define a main theme or word that best describes each grouping of attributes.

The outcome you are working towards is five to seven key ideas or values that stand out.

After you have defined five to seven groups of attributes, ask yourselves the following questions for each group:

- What would it look like (literally – what would you see people doing) if people were living out these attributes?

- What would you hear people saying if they were living out these attributes?

- What would it feel like inside the organization, if people were living out these attributes?

To make core values come alive, they have to be kinesthetic. People need to believe and feel them in everything they do.

You may want to ask a small group to take the work you have done and put together a description that defines each core value. Try and keep the descriptions to no more than two to three sentences. Many organizations use acronyms or symbols to help make their core values easy to remember.

Once your core values are defined, there are many ways to bring them to life. Some companies start every meeting by sharing stories of employees living out the core values. Other organizations talk about them regularly as a part of every team members' 1-on-1 meeting with their manager. Living out the core values is equally as important as every employees' responsibilities and goals, so you must be talking about them.

Bring up your core values in your recruiting process by asking candidates probing questions. For example, if one of your core values is integrity, ask the candidate to about when their integrity was challenged and how they handled it.

ROCK & SAND

Core Values: Mission to Mars

FOUR DECISIONS® Tools

The 5-7 passengers on the *Mission to Mars* rocket that best represent your culture:

- High credibility with peers
- Most competent in their roles
- Gut-level understanding of core values

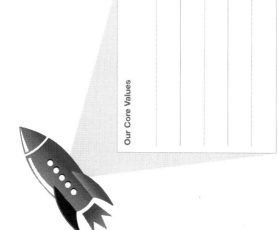

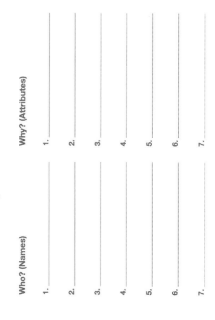

Our Core Values

Who? (Names)	Why? (Attributes)
1.	1.
2.	2.
3.	3.
4.	4.
5.	5.
6.	6.
7.	7.

Core Values Criteria

- Small set of timeless principles
- Intrinsic value and importance
- Independent of operational realities

PART TWO – IMPLEMENTING THE ROCK & SAND MODEL
CORE CUSTOMER AND BRAND PROMISE

By Carter Heim | **www.heimlantz.com**

Core Customer and Brand Promise are two more critical components of your Baseline Growth Map. Every aspect is interconnected, and each supports other aspects.

You might ask, what is a "Core Customer"? A real individual, with a unique identity and set of needs who buys at an optimal profit, pays on time, loyal and refers others, and you want more of them. The identification of your Core Customer to inform your strategy must be nuanced and robust.

Identify your Core Customer - Three steps: individual work, followed by sharing, then wrapped up into a final definition. Pull out the Core Customer Tool and pass it out to your team to guide them through these steps.

1. Individual work –
   a. List the names of three to five customers that you consider among your best customers, and who you enjoy working with.

   b. Next to each name, describe the customer, focus on the personal attributes of the person who buys from you, not the demographics of the company he or she works for – various attributes that make them a great customer.

   c. After the description of each of the customers, list your thoughts about the needs you are filling for the customer.

2. Each team member then shares the three to five customers she/he identified, their attributes, and their needs. Make sure you capture them on two lists.

3. The group then discusses what they heard and identifies the patterns and themes. From the themes, the group creates a 2 – 4 bullet point list, describing your Core Customer. Challenge the characteristics, test them, and finalize your version.

Once you identify your Core Customer it's time to create your Brand Promise. This is how you differentiate your company and its products and services from your competition. It is also how you move prospect discussions from focusing solely on price or features and benefits to needs being fulfilled. The Brand Promise becomes your strategy and drives growth Your Brand Promise is what you do differently than your competition that catches the Customer's attention and keeps it.

There are two elements to the Brand Promise. The Lead Promise and Secondary Promises. The Lead Promise articulates the main difference you deliver to your Core Customer and is usually broader in nature. The Secondary Promises articulate other differentiators that support and help convey the Lead Promise. Secondary Promises can be very specific.

During your work to identify your Core Customer you started the process of defining your Brand Promise. With your team, list all the needs you can identify for your Core Customer. Focus on the needs that go deeper than features and benefits, the needs that if satisfied really make a difference with the individual "person." Challenge your team to identify what other needs are missing, add them to the list. Then:

Each team member picks their top three needs (meaning most valuable to the customers) and indicates their votes.

1. Tabulate the votes and identify the top 10. Discuss the Top 10, challenge the value, get clear as to why each is or is not highly valuable to your customers.

2. Each team member votes for their top three of the ten 10. List your team's top five by votes.

3. Pass out the Brand Promise Tool, and ask each team member to put down their answers for what they believe the Lead Promise is, and what two of the Secondary Promises are.

4. Share their results. Dialogue deeply about the answers. Decide on the Lead Promise and Secondary Promises.

5. Test it with a few great customers. Do they care about the promise? Do you deliver in accordance with the promise?

As you move forward through this book, you'll learn how to connect the Brand Promise to what you are going to do to make sure you deliver on it.

Core Customer: Do You Know Your WHO?

FOUR DECISIONS® Tools

Attributes of your WHO (Core Customer):

- A real person with wants, needs, and fears
- Will buy for optimal profit
- Has an unique online identity and behavior
- Pays on time, loyal, and refers others
- Exists today among your customers

Each team member:

- List **names** of 5 REAL ideal customers
- Describe ONE ideal **characteristic** of each of them

Collaborate as a team:

- List your 5 core customer characteristics

1. _____

2. _____

3. _____

4. _____

5. _____

In 10-15 words, describe your Core Customer:

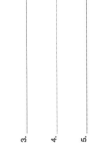

NAME

CHARACTERISTIC

NAME

CHARACTERISTIC

CORE
Customer

NAME

CHARACTERISTIC

NAME

CHARACTERISTIC

NAME

CHARACTERISTIC

ROCK & SAND

Brand Promise: Your Measurable Customer Commitment

FOUR DECISIONS® Tools

Brand Promise criteria:

- Does it differentiate you?
- Is it Measurable?
- Does it fill the right (CORE) Customers' need (not a want)?

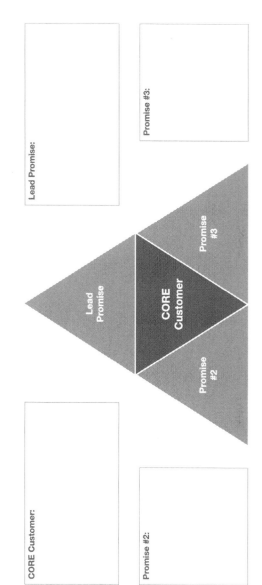

Lead Promise:

Promise #3:

CORE Customer:

Promise #2:

PART TWO – IMPLEMENTING THE ROCK & SAND MODEL
PROFIT PER X

By Glen Dall | www.apexnorthcoaching.com

Let me introduce an important concept and accompanying worksheet that comes from the work of Jim Collins' book, *Good to Great*. It's "Profit Per X: Your Company's Unique KPI for Scaling Up." "X" represents the engine of your company's most profitable growth. Think of it as the overarching Key Performance Indicator (KPI) to scale your company, profitability. This is something many companies miss. They find themselves outgrowing their available capital and plateau, or worse yet, sputter out and stall. By carefully crafting your company's Profit Per X to be a KPI that your team can impact and optimize, you will be setting your company ahead of competitors with industry leading profitability.

Profit per X can be difficult to conceptualize and develop for your own business. I'll give you a great example from one of my clients, Sara, owner of a jewelry design firm. Sara started with a retail jewelry store. Her passion and focus were for creating custom jewelry pieces that reflected the taste and style of her clients. She started with Profit per Customer as her X. By looking at this, she was able to determine that many of her showroom customers were actually costing her money by taking up time and not spending very much.

Sara closed the expensive showroom and moved to a studio in a lower-cost area, by appointment only. By serving her loyal, highest value customers by appointment, her revenue per customer soared.

One of her customers asked if she could make an appointment on a Sunday and bring three of her friends, Sara offered to supply hors d'oeuvres and mimosas. All four ended up ordering custom jewelry, resulting in 4X the normal revenue of an appointment. Guess what Sara's new X is? Revenue per appointment! Much like Southwest airlines is one of the one profitable US airlines from focusing on keeping its planes in the air full of customers, Sara can greatly drive the success of her business by optimizing her appointments.

Work with your leadership team and use the Profit Per X Tool to discover potential Profit Per Xs. Pass out the tool to each team member. Have them work brainstorm individually and document their suggestions on what the X could be. Come together as a team and do a deep dialogue on the answers and decide on two potential Xs from all the suggestions. Start tracking the two over the next several months to see which works best.

The Profit Per X should also help you decide on your BHAG or "Big Hairy Audacious Goal," that you will work on in the next chapter.

Cheers to your profitable growth!

Profit Per X: Your Company's Unique KPI for Scaling Up

ROCK & SAND

FOUR DECISIONS® Tools

Attributes of your Profit Per X:

- Single overarching KPI to scale your business
- Fundamental economic engine of your business

- Able to impact and optimize both revenue and cost of "X"
- Tightly aligns with your BHAG® (use same unit of measurement)

$$\text{Fundamental Economic Engine (Scalable)} = \frac{\text{PROFIT}}{\text{X}}$$

"Profit"   This is an important financial unit that drives profit (e.g. gross profit, revenue, net profit)

"X"   This is your fundamental building block for scaling the business, which you can act on to increase revenue and lower cost (e.g. airplanes, deliveries, clients)

Instructions:

- Each team member brainstorms individually
- Collaborate as a team to select two potential "profit" metrics and "X" building blocks
- Remember, your "X" should be consistent with your BHAG®

Profit KPI	"X" Building Block
Profit KPI	"X" Building Block

PART TWO – IMPLEMENTING THE ROCK & SAND MODEL
BIG HAIRY AUDACIOUS GOAL

By Glen Dall | www.apexnorthcoaching.com

"BHAG," short for Big Hairy Audacious Goal, was coined by Jim Collins and Jerry Porras in their book Built to Last: Successful Habits of Visionary Companies. They state that a clear and compelling "BHAG, serves as unifying focal point of effort, and acts as a clear catalyst for team spirit. It has a clear finish line, so the organization can know when it has achieved the goal; people like to shoot for finish lines."

I prefer to think of BHAG as the North Star that guides your long-term vision for yourself and your business. I also use the metaphor of the mountain peak you want to climb. I believe so greatly in it that I named my coaching practice "Apex North" to embody it.

Your BHAG® should be BIG, almost unreachable. It should be long-term, many times as much as 10 to 20, or even 30 years out. It should be HAIRY, which means hard to do. It should be AUDACIOUS, which means bold, something that at first you're almost afraid to say out loud for fear of being laughed at. And of course, it needs to be phrased as a GOAL.

If you've done a good job of defining your Core Purpose, Profit Per X, and Brand Promise from the previous chapters, you have the foundation to develop your BHAG using the "The BHAG Tool." Talk as a team about the three intersecting circles on the guide. What are you passionate about, what are you good at, and what is the Profit Per X that drives your business? The intersection of the three circles is where you will find your BHAG.

Don't worry if you don't get it right away. This is something that takes time. Focus on the BIG part of the BHAG and at least get that down and let the idea of the goal percolate in the minds of your team for a while, maybe several months. Try to tie it to the difference you are making in the world as defined in your Core Purpose so that the BHAG is not purely monetary and will be meaningful to your entire team.

One classic example of this was a BHAG developed by President John F. Kennedy in 1962. At that time the United States was lagging behind the Soviet Union in space exploration and the associated technology, and Kennedy's presidential administration had been damaged by a botched covert military attack on Cuba by a CIA-sponsored group.

While initially facing strong resistance from Congress and the American people, Kennedy was able to capture the hearts and imagination of the nation with a BHAG of putting a man on the moon within 10 years. He unveiled it in a speech with the tagline "We choose to go to the moon!" In July of 1969, Apollo 11 landed on the moon for the first time ever. The impossible had become possible.

That's exactly what a BHAG® should be. Inspiring, exciting, almost not attainable. It's that shining star that when things are dark, the journey long and tiring, you will lift your head to see that vision, it will renew your strength and propel you further down your path to greatness.

How will you know when you've fond your BHAG®, your North Star? When you say it out loud, and you feel a chill, or get goosebumps, and have to say aloud again, with growing determination, because it's just so. Damn. Great. It will feel like you can't wait to put your own person on the moon.

The BHAG®: Your 10 to 30-Year North Star

FOUR DECISIONS® Tools

Big Hairy Audacious Goal (BHAG®) attributes:

- Arises from the Hedgehog overlap
- Challenges you to greatness
- Reinforces business fundamentals

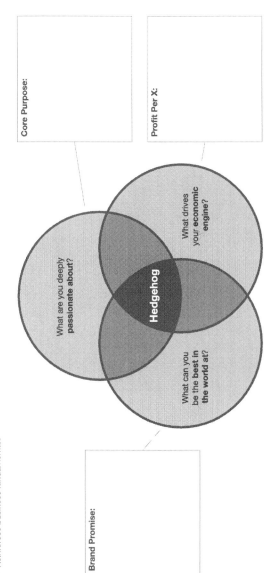

Core Purpose:

Profit Per X:

What are you deeply passionate about?

What drives your economic engine?

What can you be the best in the world at?

Hedgehog

Brand Promise:

PART TWO — IMPLEMENTING THE ROCK & SAND MODEL
STRATEGIC TARGETS

By Adam Siegel | **www.visageinvest.com**

Before you start using the "Strategic Targets" tool, I suggest that you do a review of your current business model (strengths and weaknesses) against the prevailing and/or potential market trends. There are numerous methods to do this. The point is that your team understand the challenges that need to be addressed for your businesses to grow and thrive, protect its current market(s), and leverage its strengths, and take this information and apply it to setting the strategic targets.

The "Strategic Targets" tool is a method that helps you set the context for where you want to be three to five years out, clarifies the major performance marks you need to achieve along the way, AND energizes our team to achieve these targets. As with any goal, we need to ensure that these targets are achievable, measurable, and timebound. Establishing these with your leadership team is critical to achieve business engagement AND generate multiple perspectives from your trusted leaders.

Some businesses are comfortable setting a timeframe of about five years. However, many businesses find that they cannot stretch their thinking long enough to project out that long. And while setting our Strategic Targets is NOT about being precise in predicting the future, a three year time is horizon deemed most appropriate. In fact rapidly evolving industries tend to struggle with even 3 year time horizons.

There are numerous ways to set targets, but we have a simple approach which entails the following steps:

1. Thinking about your business in 3 years (in the context of its market), brainstorm with your leadership team, the top targets or performance indicators that you would like your business lined up to deliver against. Revenue ($), Gross Profit ($), EBITDA ($), Number of Sales (units), Cash at Bank are some fairly typical targets used. Other targets may include, employee numbers, number of channel partners, Net Promoter Scores, Employee Net Promoter Score,

Production Efficiency, various safety measures, and Market Share. NOTE: you want these targets to be "strategic" targets i.e., those outcomes that represent the high level performance of your business, and are not too granular.

2. For the strategic targets you have set, brainstorm and agree with your team the specific targets to be achieved in three years' time, and insert them in the year three column on the tool.

3. Once you have this recorded, with your team, agree what each target will need to be at the two year, and then the one year mark…

For the advanced and adventurous businesses, AND for those planning to grow their markets, develop more products/service offerings, or diversify, you can run the same process as above for each of the new stream(s) in your business.

In setting these strategic targets, you can expect to have some rigorous debate. This is a good thing! In the end, remember, this is not about predicting the future. This is about inspiring your organization to achieve exceptional outcomes and having a clear and measured path to achieving long term success!

ROCK & SAND

Strategic Targets: Aiming for Success

FOUR DECISIONS® Tools

	Year 1	Year 2	Year 3	Year 4	Year 5
Financial Target #1 **Total Revenue**					
Current Offerings Revenue					
. . .					
New Offerings Revenue					
. . .					
Strategic Target #2					
Strategic Target #3					
Strategic Target #4					
Strategic Target #5					

PART TWO – IMPLEMENTING THE ROCK & SAND MODEL
KEY THRUSTS

By Lynn Hartrick | **www.hartrickleadership.com**

Determining Key Thrusts and Capabilities is a key component of the intermediate planning that leaders need to put in place to bridge the gaps between the longer-term goal (BHAG) and the nearer term goals (Annual Initiatives). This intermediate planning has more to do with setting direction than it does setting specific goals. The intermediate planning reflects the strategic direction in which the company is heading over the next three years.

The previous chapter explained how to set three Year Targets that align with the progress necessary to achieve the BHAG. Once the financial targets are completed, an obvious question remains. How is the company going to achieve these forecasts over the next 3 years? What capabilities must be developed or acquired? What capabilities are missing that must be supplied? What winning moves must be made regarding geographic expansion or new product development or talent acquisition? To name just a few areas for consideration. In short, what are the key necessary thrusts, or strategic chess moves, the company must make if it is to claim success three years from now?

Key Thrusts: Your Three Year Chess Moves

You've downloaded the Key Thrusts Tool that can be used by leaders and advisory boards to help answer this question. It is based around the Four Decisions Model. (People, Strategy, Execution and Cash). The objective of the exercise is to identify Three to Five Key Thrusts to be the strategic focus for the next 3 years.

Step 1

It is important to have the right people participating in this exercise. This may be your leadership team, or it may be key advisors with particular experience or strategic thinking skills. Still another alternative may be to invite key employees because of their particular experience or knowledge of the business. Or it may be some combination of these people. What is important is to get the best collective strategic thinking possible to generate the most viable outcomes. The number of participants should be kept relatively small. Six is ideal and, certainly, no more than eight.

Step 2

Preparation for this exercise may include a review of the planning work completed to this point. In particular, all participants in the exercise should be fully aware of the completed three targets including financial forecasts such as Revenue and Gross Margin targets. For sure, the participants should review the BHAG and be familiar with the Profit/X metric developed to measure it. And it would be beneficial to review productivity targets as well as any targets set for team talent. Once all has been reviewed and understanding reached, you are ready to proceed to step 3.

Step 3

Hand out the exercise and ask each participant to work individually to identify two key chess moves (thrusts/strategic actions) for each of the four decision areas.

Step 4

Bring the group back together and have individuals share their ideas and post them on a white board. When all participants have shared and debated, have the group combine the lists and select the Top Two chess moves for each decision area.

Step 5

Now with the top two chess moves selected in each decision area, have the group select the top three to five moves from all the selected chess moves. These are your thrusts/strategic actions for the next three years.

ROCK & SAND

Key Thrusts: Your 3 to 5-Year Chess Moves

FOUR DECISIONS® Tools

Review your 3-5 year targets:

* Revenue
* Gross margin
* BHAG®
* Profit Per X
* Labor productivity
* Team talent

Each team member:

* Develop 2 key thrusts (strategic actions over a 3-5 year time frame) that will position you to achieve your targets

Collaborate as a team:

* Rank the top 2 "chess moves" in each of the Four Decisions™
* Select and circle your top 5 key thrusts for the next 3-5 years

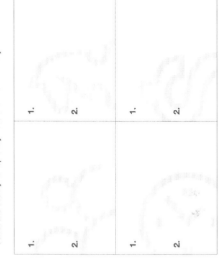

PART TWO — IMPLEMENTING THE ROCK & SAND MODEL
CRITICAL NUMBER

By Rick Holbrook | **www.growthstratagems.com**

Even though we haven't yet created a "Critical Number Tool," we feel the concept of "Critical Number" is important to picking and moving Rocks. It's being developed so check back in in the future to download it. "Critical Number" and other practices of Open Book Management are more fully documented in Jack Stack's book, The Great Game of Business *and its companion guide,* Get in the Game *by Rich Armstrong and Steve Baker, which has evolved into a coaching and training firm supporting companies on the practices of Open Book Management. The Great Game of Business[©] is a strategic partner of Gravitas Impact Premium Coaches –Synk*

In 1983 Jack Stack and some colleagues scraped together $100,000, borrowed $8.9 Million and completed the buyout of the Springfield Re-Manufacturing division from International Harvester. Seeing only $100,000 of owner's equity invested in the business, the lenders were very nervous and Jack realized the company's survival depended on reducing this debt. Using their 89:1 debt to equity ratio as the critical number they had to improve, and with the rallying cry of "debt to equity = job security" Jack focused everyone on reducing the debt.

By the end of 1984 they had reduced their debt to $2.5M, saved the company and positioned it for long term success by having fixed their #1 weakness. From this experience Jack realized the power of attacking and fixing the #1 weakness in the company and engaging everyone in doing that through improving the critical number that represented it. Thus, was born the concept of the critical number against which people can keep score and experience the joy of winning.

To find the critical number at your company, you first must find the one big thing, that if fixed within a year, will significantly improve your business. Ask yourself, your employees and other stakeholders, "If we could fix one thing by the end of the year what should it be?", "What's an area of weakness or opportunity for our company?", "What opportunity if captured will move us ahead of our competition?".

For example, a company might identify cash flow problems or revenue growth as their critical weakness to fix. Once the weakness is found and agreed upon the next step is to find the key activities that drive that result. Some examples:

- For poor cash flow, it might be collecting faster, reducing mistakes, or reducing inventory.

- A company that needs to grow its revenue might focus on increasing the number of referrals or online demo's or whatever sales actions drives their revenue.

Once the activities are identified, the next step is to calculate the current (unacceptable) level of those activities and from that number, figure out the critical number for each that represents success.

- For the example of improving cash flow, if the current collections are 85 days, you might set a target critical number of 60 days. This is the number to relentlessly communicate to your people and track via a visible scoreboard or game.

Once the critical number is known, all employees should set their priorities and actions to align with improving that number. If everyone is focused on attacking and fixing a critical weakness, you're building a stronger foundation for growth. Some tips for picking a critical number:

- **make it real:** Use the critical number to educate your people on your business with the long-term goal being to train them to think like business owners.

- **make it win/win:** Share the savings when they beat the number.

- **make it fun:** People love to compete and exceed a number. Tap into their competitive spirit

- **make it relevant:** get each department to contribute to achieving the critical number.

PART TWO – IMPLEMENTING THE ROCK & SAND MODEL
ANNUAL INITIATIVES

By Robert Clinkenbeard | **www.theradixgroupllc.com**

Setting three to five clear annual initiatives can be one of the single most crucial difference whether your company grows or not.

Many company leaders often confuse annual budgeting or short-term action steps with yearly planning. Other leaders struggle to think big picture, and this often leads to stunted growth. Some of the other poor traits I stumble upon regularly include:

- Over ambition – owners can often list all the issues they are aware of in the company, and then they will turn them into "annual priorities." Unfortunately, the list can be as many as 15 – 20 when it is best practice to have 3 -5 annual priorities. I prefer 3.

- Failure to recognize the trends – leaders occasionally let their ego influence their decision making. Just because a tried and tested formula has worked in the past doesn't necessarily mean it will be successful in the future.

- Putting on the blinders – some companies struggle to scale as they don't take risks, set stretch goals and focus too much on fixing all the company weaknesses or issues. On the other end of the spectrum ignoring your shortcomings can lead to unhappy clients, significant financial losses or disgruntled employees. Every company should make it a priority to seriously address, if not eliminate, at least one weakness per year.

- Lack of clarity and communication – Many owners and their advisors often lock themselves away for a day or two towards the end of the year to work on annual planning. On completion, they either keep it to themselves, or they struggle to communicate it clearly to their whole team. Getting your leadership team involved in the planning process will encourage buy-in, develop a culture of accountability and will help to communicate a clear, aligned vision throughout the company.

It is essential to follow these steps in preparing your 3 – 5 annual initiatives:

1. Review with your team as much as you can about your company and the market place. Include such things as client surveys, employee surveys, SWOT (Strengths, Weaknesses, Opportunities, Threats) analysis, and Start, Stop, Keep Surveys.

2. Review what has been completed thus far in completing your Baseline Growth Roadmap, especially the Three Year Key Thrusts that were developed in the previous chapter, to make sure your annual initiative line up well with them.

3. Review what your company's Critical Number is so you can make sure the initiatives improve that number. Your top priority should tie in directly with your leading Critical Number.

4. Give the Annual Initiatives Tool to your team. Ask them to fill it out individually, writing down what they see the initiatives being, in light of what they have reviewed in the three previous steps.

5. Then bring them together and have them present their answers to the group. Facilitate a "sorting out" discussion of all the answers and prioritize them for importance, urgency and alignment.

6. Document your final decisions on the Baseline Growth Roadmap.

When you put these practices in place, combined with a solid execution plan and a rhythm of productive meetings, you have taken some massively important steps towards having a successful year.

ROCK & SAND

Annual Initiatives: Top 5 and "First of Five"

FOUR DECISIONS® Tools

Instructions:

- As a team, identify and finalize your critical number(s)
- Individually, draft your company's top 5 priorities using your One-Page Strategic Plan as guidance
- As a team, debate and finalize the top 5 company priorities
- Using critical numbers as a guide, highlight your top priority "First of Five"
- Set personal accountability and completion date for each priority

Top 5 Priorities: Annual Initiatives

		LEADER	DATE
1.			
2.			
3.			
4.			
5.			

PART TWO – IMPLEMENTING THE ROCK & SAND MODEL
QUARTERLY ROCKS

By Will Ditzler | **www.riverbirchadvisors.com**

We all know the difficulty in maintaining focus on the things that matter most. With all the sand filling coming at us, it is critical that we, as leaders, filter priorities down to the top three to five and the number one. This applies to longer-term strategic moves, one-year key initiatives, quarterly priorities and even to each week and day.

As coaches, one of the execution disciplines that we see make the biggest difference in our client's success is developing quarterly priorities or "Rocks" to drive results within the context of your One Page Strategic Plan and meeting rhythms.

Give each executive team member a copy of the "Quarterly Rocks" tool you downloaded earlier. Have them first review your Key Thrusts, Annual Initiatives as well as your current performance numbers. Have each executive team member independently write down up to 5 things they feel are the most important things that need to get accomplished in the next 90 days to meet your goals and continue on your path up the mountain toward your Big Hairy Audacious Goal (BHAG), Three Year and Annual Targets, and Annual Goals. Write all of them up on a white board and then have the team rank them into the top 3 using the following questions as a filter:

1. Is it one of the most important things we can do in the next 90 days?

2. Is it not likely to get done or get done well if we don't make it a rock?

3. Is there something that needs to be done first (another rock) to insure it can be completed?

4. Does it require or benefit from a team approach or collective intelligence vs. an individual priority?

Once you've identified your top three rocks for the coming quarter:

1. Choose one person from the executive team to be accountable for moving each rock. (WHO)

2. Document rocks on your Baseline Growth Roadmap including the WHO.

3. Rock leaders choose their rock team and set up a meeting within 2 weeks of the quarterly planning session. The rock team can and should often include others in the organization who may not be on the executive team, but usually only an executive team member can be accountable for the rock.

4. During this meeting, clearly define a WRITTEN PURPOSE STATEMENT for the rock, as well as specific deliverables and a timeframe for each deliverable.

5. Each rock leader gives a brief update in the weekly meetings (1 minute) and a more substantive update at the monthly meetings (10 minutes) to drive accountability.

6. At each quarterly, the rocks are presented with a summary of what was accomplished and any remaining action items (Who, What and When)

7. New rocks are chosen for the next quarter.

Like many other things in life, the difference between using rocks well and not is in the details and discipline. In implementing hundreds of rocks as a CEO and Coach in the last 15 years, this is the system I have found to be the most effective in consistently accomplishing quarterly priorities.

Quarterly Rocks: Top 3 to 5 Priorities

FOUR DECISIONS® Tools

Instructions:

- As a team, identify and finalize your critical number(s)
- Individually, draft your company's top 3 to 5 priorities using your One-Page Strategic Plan as guidance
- As a team, debate and finalize the top 3 to 5 company priorities
- Using critical numbers as a guide, highlight your top priority
- Set personal accountability and completion date for each priority

Top 3 to 5 Priorities: Quarterly Priorities

1.		LEADER	DATE
2.		LEADER	DATE
3.		LEADER	DATE
4.		LEADER	DATE
5.		LEADER	DATE

PART TWO – IMPLEMENTING THE ROCK & SAND MODEL
MEETING RHYTHM

By Rick Holbrook | **www.growthstratagems.com**

Poor communication is a direct result of poor meeting habits and while individual meetings can be improved, we've found the larger issue is that most companies lack the framework of meetings that will enable them to achieve their rocks. Also, because they haven't intentionally designed a meeting rhythm, every department leader does their own thing, which leads to a proliferation of ad-hoc, inefficient, inconsistent and disconnected meetings, in other words, meeting bloat.

A well-designed meeting rhythm is the execution habit that moves both the rocks and sand. It promotes transparency and accountability, improves communication, provides a format for continual education and learning, and most importantly maintains focus on the Rocks and the company's critical number. Here is an overview of the framework we recommend:

Daily Huddle:

- Once a day at same time, 12 minutes max

- All employees participate by department/team; no one in more than 2 daily huddles

- Agenda: Good News/What's Up, Metrics/Commitment updates; Obstacles/Stucks; Top to do for day; Closing Thoughts

- Do's: be prepared; make attendance mandatory; stand only; things

- Don'ts: try to solve issues (set up one off meetings to solve them), no opting out, sit; exceed max time

- Benefits: Better morale, better communication; saves time; identify people's obstacles and daily priority

Weekly Meeting:

- Once a week at same time for 60 – 90 minutes; all employees participate by department/team, no one in more than 2 weekly meetings

- Agenda: Good News; Review status of Rocks (Green/Yellow/ Red); Share Feedback: Market, Competitor, Customers, employee; Select & Resolve 1-2 most important tactical obstacles & issues

- Do: keep it tactical; list then select most important obstacle/ issue for resolution by the team and try to solve it; Engage in healthy debate on the topics; record action item by who and by when;

- Don'ts: no strategic topics; don't wait to set agenda until after the meeting starts

- Benefits: solve bigger tasks not solve able between daily huddles; identify status of rocks; engage team in solving high priority issues or help those who's priorities are lagging; make adjustments to stay on plan; identify issues or opportunities for decision at monthly meeting

Monthly Strategic:

- Once a month at consistent day and time for 2 to 4 hours; attended by leadership team with mid-level managers if applicable

- Agenda: Review monthly results (financials and/or non-financial metrics); Review progress vs quarterly Rocks & course correct; Review 2 max operational obstacles/choke points or Strategic topics

- Do: Engage in healthy conflict on the topics; Push for group accountability; Learn something

- Don't: Tackle too many issues; Pick 2 topics until after review and update

- Benefits: identify and solve bigger issues elevated from the weekly meetings; Identify and discuss issues flagged as strategic in weekly meeting; identify issues to be resolved at quarterly planning meeting

Quarterly Meeting
- Once a quarter for 1 or 2 days; attended by leadership team to
  - o Review last quarter's results
  - o Educate team on relevant topic or skills;
  - o Adjust plan based on learnings;
  - o Plan for next quarter, (Set Rocks)

- Agenda: review last quarter vs goals and rocks; summarize key learnings & adjust strategy as required; Educational component for leadership team; set priorities, accountabilities and theme for next quarter

- Do: focus on work; limit social agenda; prioritize top 1 of 1 for each person

- Don't: set overly ambitious schedule; forget to share the plan with everyone's teams

- Benefits: prepare executable quarterly plan with accountabilities and timelines; ensure alignment with longer term plans; provide format for continuing executive education

Annual Meeting
- Once a year for 1-2 days; attended by leadership team

ROCK & SAND

Meeting Rhythms: Setting the Organizational Heartbeat

FOUR DECISIONS® Tools

Communication Rhythm Action Plan:

- The top challenge in any organization is communication
- A series of 5 ongoing meetings will bring focus, alignment and save time
- Commit to a specific meeting schedule to establish communication rhythm

Individually:

- Suggest best times and dates for the 5 meeting rhythms

Date	Day of Week	Time
DAILY HUDDLE		5 - 15 MINS
WEEKLY MEETING		60 - 90 MINS
MONTHLY MANAGEMENT MEETING		4 - 8 HOURS
QUARTERLY PLANNING		1 - 2 DAYS
ANNUAL PLANNING		1 - 3 DAYS

As a leadership team:

- Collaborate, choose, and calendar each meeting for the entire year

YEAR

	Time	Day	Date(s)
Daily Huddle			
Weekly Meeting			
Monthly Meeting			
Quarterly Planning			
Pre-Annual Planning			
Annual Planning			

PART TWO – IMPLEMENTING THE ROCK & SAND MODEL

THE UPWARD EVOLUTION PRINCIPLE: FORWARD MOTION OVER PERFECTION

By Keith Cupp, CEO/Head Coach, Gravitas Impact Premium Coaches
www.gicoaches.com

Congratulations, you have just learned how to use some of the most powerful tools to clarify, focus, and activate your business, non-profit or community organization. In the process, we have encouraged you to not only learn, but also apply each tool to your organization as part of the process to create positive change and unleash growth. One of the best attributes of the tools is that they are dynamic and can be continuously applied to the growth of your organization through time and changing circumstances.

First a quick review, the process to put the use of Rock & Sand and Gravitas Tools:

1. **Learn:** Read the Rock & Sand book.

2. **Apply:** Activate the principles by completing the Baseline Growth Roadmap.

3. **Evolve:** Ensure your upward growth through continuous reapplication.

As our coaches work with and listen to their clients worldwide, we are hearing a consistent "thread of success" across the globe. We refer to it as "The Upward Evolution Principle."

Here is how to activate that principle with what you have learned:

1. **Rough** Out: Learn and apply the Rock & Sand Model and Gravitas Tools in your organization to an 80% "good enough" outcome. Do your best to rough out your Baseline Growth Roadmap using your initial knowledge of the model and tools. This may feel awkward, uncomfortable and slow. That's okay!

2. **Refine:** Relearn and reapply the model and tools in your organization to a 95% "much better" outcome. Use your experience with the principles and tools to refine and improve your Baseline Growth Roadmap. This will increase your confidence, and deliver progress and results. That's wonderful!

3. **Arrive:** Skillfully refine the reapplication of the model and tools to a 98% "well honed" outcome. Use the expertise you have developed in executing your business through time to become outstanding as you dial in your Baseline Growth Roadmap. This will elicit feelings of mastery, expertise and great risk tolerance to growth. You have arrived!

Why only 80% to start? Forward motion with application of the model and tools is infinitely more important than seeking perfection and delay. Give yourselves, as leaders, permission to "learn, fail forward and refine."

Why only 98% to finish? There is no perfection in continuous reapplication of the model and tools; there is only the pursuit of excellence, and a 2% "always learning" process.

How long do these cycles take? It depends. The answer is directly related to your willingness to learn, take risks, iterate, refine and reapply.

This second edition of Rock & Sand has been written by some of the world's greatest mid-market coaches and is designed to help you get started on your own. However, the speed of upward evolution will be greatly increased by using a Certified Coach who has worked with many other companies to catalyze their success using this model and tools. Feel free to reach out to us at www.gicoaches. com to be introduced to a Certified Coach who can help you.

One last request. Please pick up a copy of Rock & Sand and give it to the Non-Profit leader of your choice. You (and they) will be glad you did!

ACKNOWLEDGEMENTS

Rock and Sand was a collaborative work born out of frustration: mine, and that of my clients.

I would work with my clients, in many different formats, to create clever, clear strategic plans. My clients bought into them and they were effective in creating direction for their organizations. Their teams bought into them as well and were generally pretty excited about them.

Still, in almost every case, execution was a problem. Teams would agree on an action to improve the company for the next ninety days, then go back to their day to day routines and set the action aside. That or they tried to do too many actions at one time, making progress on none, and then default to their previous personal routines.

I was frustrated, they were frustrated.

We all liked the idea of "moving a rock" even though we didn't really understand it. We repeatedly discussed and explored the imagery of moving rocks. I wore out numerous flipcharts drawing out pictures of what we discussed. Finally, one of the pictures resonated. At an executive briefing, I dropped the usual material I present and drew the latest version of the Rock and Sand drawing. It resonated unanimously among those attending, all business owners. Not satisfied with one encounter of this type, I tried it out on numerous people, individually and in groups. I made a couple of fairly unprofessional videos of the idea and shared them.

The most common comment was, "I finally get this," followed by either a sigh of relief if they thought they were working on rocks and sand, or more likely a pained expression when they realized they weren't really moving their business forward.

I have a number of people to thank for their part in creating this idea and the subsequent video and book: Ron Huntington, Keith Cupp, and all the talented coaches at Gravitas Premium Impact Coaches, all of my clients over the past 15 years from In-Synk, Inner Circle, and Clarity Council; Trace Hallowell of Tactical Magic, who pushed me to frame out these ideas in a more professional manner than I would have on my own; Mark Green, Eric Mathews, Tara McAdams, and Ron Huntington, who each helped me shape the first edition in critical ways, while always paying attention to the sensitivities of my ego; Andi Crawford-Andrus and Maureen Chan-Heflin who helped with important design elements of the book.

I'm especially grateful for the contributions of the nine Gravitas Impact Premium Coach peers who shared their expertise to explain how to use the Gravitas Implementation Tools to implement the Rock & Sand Model. They are Chris Kenny, Kirsti Tcherkoyan, Carter Heim, Glen Dall, Adam Siegel, Lynn Hartwick, Rick Holbrook, Robert Clinkenbeard, Will Ditzler, and Keith Cupp. I'm forever grateful and learned so much from all of you in the process.

And as always, I am thankful for the love and support of my wife and family, without which I really couldn't accomplish anything.

– Michael Synk

ABOUT THE AUTHOR

After establishing himself as a successful businessperson over a twenty-year career, Michael Synk has spent the 17 years as a business educator, coach and consultant. He is one of the original sixteen coaches in North America certified by Gravitas Premium Impact Coaches to teach and facilitate the highly successful Four Decisions™ curriculum which uses the Baseline Growth Roadmap™.

> *"Hard data and my own personal experience reveal that if you effectively align your strategies, actions and goals, you will be in a stronger position to leverage efficiency and growth. Everything we do is geared toward giving our executive clients the clarity they need to succeed."*

Michael graduated from the University of Michigan. He taught social studies and coached sports at Catholic High Schools in the city of Detroit for two years.

Embarking on a business career in the temporary help and health care practice industries, after 20 years, in 2000, he started his coaching practice, In-Synk: Aligning Strategy Actions and Goals. He joined Gravitas Impact Premium Coaches in 2003 and is the second longest tenured coach in the organization.

This is Michael's second book, the first being *How to Create Customer as Loyal as Norm Peterson, The Cheers Model of Marketing*, a funny and entertaining look at customer loyalty and what it takes to build it.

He is currently working on a third book, a leadership memoir of his one season as a track coach at Holy Redeemer High School in Southwest Detroit in 1980

Michael has been married for over 30 years, has three children, and resides with his family in Memphis, Tennessee.

THE CO-AUTHORS

Chris Kenny

Chris inspires purpose-driven leaders to bring their vision to life by giving them the clarity they need to make great decisions. He is an experienced business lawyer, entrepreneur and Certified Gravitas Impact Coach based in Albuquerque, New Mexico.

Kirsti Tcherkoyan

Kirsti is the CEO of 20/20 Insights, a coaching firm focused on connecting people and strategy. Her favorite thing to coach teams on is how to make sure every player knows their position, what they need to do to be successful and how each player makes a difference. Kirsti is based in San Francisco and spends a lot of time growing entrepreneurs in East Africa.

Carter Heim

Carter is the CEO and a founder of HeimLantz CPAs & Advisors, LLC, a full service advisory and accounting firm serving privately held businesses and their owners for over 30 years. Carter works with the leadership teams to identify and clarify their strategy and to build sustainable, growing companies. The firm has offices in Annapolis & Lexington Park, Maryland and Alexandria, Virginia.

Glen Dall

Glen Dall, CEO is a successful CEO with an inspiring personal story and hard-won experience stepping in to lead the turnaround and growth of a publicly-traded company. Today Glen is the founder and CEO of Apex North Business Coaching based in Minneapolis. From better to best, Apex North picks up where consultants, business groups, and frameworks like EOS leave off.

Adam Siegel

Adam is the CEO of Visage Growth Partners based in Melbourne, Australia. Leveraging his 20+ years corporate executive experience, Adam now works with growth focused CEOs and business owners across Australia and South-East Asia, helping them demystify growth and ease the pain that can come with scaling a business. A father of 4 children, Adam has been learning to be a DJ (!!) over the last few years, and still holds a dream that when he hits the age of 55 he will join US Seniors Golf circuit.

Lynn Hartrick

Lynn is Founder and Principal of Hartrick Leadership, LLC which offers Executive Coaching and Business Advisory services to mid-market firms. The business is located in Rochester, NY and has been servicing clients around the USA for over 20 years.

Rick Holbrook

Rick is the founder and owner of Growth Stratagems. His business leverages his 25 years of corporate experience with high growth rate companies where he held executive level responsibility for sales, marketing, engineering and international business development. He has experienced firsthand the challenges and successes of growing a business and has been coaching and facilitating leadership and business growth in Western Canada since 2004.

Robert Clinkenbeard

Robert is the CEO of The Radix Group, LLC which has offices in Greenville, Phoenix and the UK. He is an entrepreneur, an author, senior leader in EO and a four time Ironman. The Radix Group will help you get a higher business valuation, reinvigorated passion for your business, extra time with family and friends, growth of your key employees, more time to work ON your business and a company culture that adopts the vision as if it were their own.

Will Ditzler

Will is President and founder of RiverBirch Executive Advisors and a certified Gravitas Impact Coach. He has been helping CEOs and leaders achieve excellence and fulfill their vision for 6 years in coaching. His passion is in building health teams and cultures and implementing execution disciplines. Prior to coaching he was President and CEO of Cardno JFNew, a leading ecological consulting, restoration and native plant nursery firm. As a member of 1% for The Planet, RiverBirch Executive Advisors donates 1% of its gross revenues to environmental and conservation organizations.

Keith Cupp

Keith is a senior coach and leader in Gravitas Impact Premium Coaches, and has been coaching mid-market companies for the past decade, many of which have been recognized as award winners in areas of culture, financial results, and business impact in their industries. With Chief Executive Officer, Thought Leader, International Business and Coaching experience, Keith brings unique insights, expertise and value to business leaders and their companies. During his service on the USS Enterprise in the United States Navy, Keith was awarded the Naval Achievement Medal, and is passionate for the cause of Freedom: Spiritual, Intellectual, Economic and Political.

GRAVITAS TOOLS APPENDIX

All tools can be downloaded at:

www.gravitasimpact.com/rockandsand

BASELINE Growth Roadmap™

FOUNDATION		3 YEARS	
CORE	**STRATEGY**	**TARGETS**	
Core Purpose	BHAG®	3HAG™	
		Year	
		Revenue	
		Gross Profit	
		Cash	
Core Values	Profit Per X	Widget 1	
		Widget 2	
		Widget 3	
	Core Customer	Key Thrusts	
		1	
		2	
		3	
Core Strengths	Brand Promise	3HAG™ Critical Numbers	
		•	
		•	
		•	

Organization:		ROCK & SAND	G
Name:	Date:		

1 YEAR	90 DAYS

GOALS	ACTIONS	PERSONAL PLAN

1HAG

Year	
Revenue	
Gross Profit	
Cash	
Widget 1	
Widget 2	
Widget 3	

90-Day Plan

Quarter	
Revenue	
Gross Profit	
Cash	
Widget 1	
Widget 2	
Widget 3	

Personal Critical Number

1

2

3

4

Annual Priorities

1

2

3

Quarterly Priorities   Who

1

2

3

Personal Priorities

1

2

3

1HAG Critical Numbers

-
-
-

Critical Numbers

-
-
-

Personal Development

-
-
-

ROCK & SAND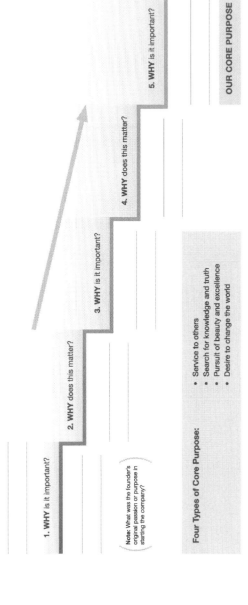

Core Purpose: Your Company's Reason for Being

FOUR DECISIONS® Tools

Attributes of a company's Core Purpose:

* Higher purpose (beyond profit and jobs)
* Does not change...but inspires change
* Engages team members emotionally
* Causes team to work around/through obstacles

Descriptive Statement

"What does your company do today"

1. WHY is it important?

2. WHY does this matter?

3. WHY is it important?

4. WHY does this matter?

5. WHY is it important?

Note: What was the founder's original passion or purpose in starting the company?

Four Types of Core Purpose:

* Service to others
* Search for knowledge and truth
* Pursuit of beauty and excellence
* Desire to change the world

OUR CORE PURPOSE

ROCK & SAND

Core Values: Mission to Mars

FOUR DECISIONS® Tools

The 5-7 passengers on the *Mission to Mars* rocket that best represent your culture:

- High credibility with peers
- Most competent in their roles
- Gut-level understanding of core values

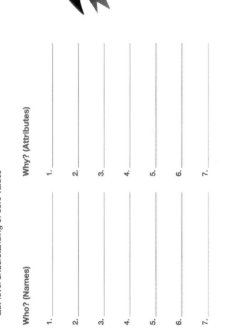

Our Core Values

Who? (Names)	Why? (Attributes)
1.	1.
2.	2.
3.	3.
4.	4.
5.	5.
6.	6.
7.	7.

Core Values Criteria

- Small set of timeless principles
- Intrinsic value and importance
- Independent of operational realities

ROCK & SAND

Core Customer: Do You Know Your WHO?

FOUR DECISIONS® Tools

Attributes of your WHO (Core Customer):

- A real person with wants, needs, and fears
- Will buy for optimal profit
- Has an unique online identity and behavior

- Pays on time, loyal, and refers others
- Exists today among your customers

Collaborate as a team:

- List your 5 core customer characteristics

1. _____

2. _____

3. _____

4. _____

5. _____

Each team member:

- List names of 5 REAL ideal customers
- Describe ONE ideal **characteristic** of each of them

NAME
CHARACTERISTIC

NAME
CHARACTERISTIC

CORE Customer

NAME
CHARACTERISTIC

NAME
CHARACTERISTIC

NAME
CHARACTERISTIC

In 10-15 words, describe your Core Customer:

_____

ROCK & SAND

Brand Promise: Your Measurable Customer Commitment

FOUR DECISIONS® Tools

Brand Promise criteria:

- Does it differentiate you?
- Is it Measurable?
- Does it fill the right (CORE) Customers' need (not a want)?

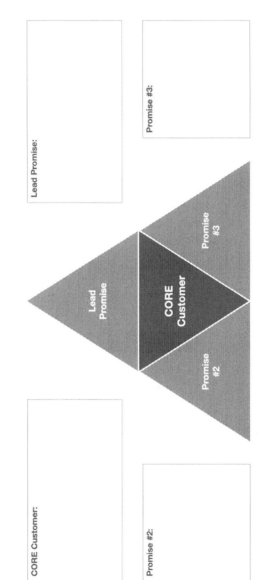

Lead Promise:

Promise #3:

CORE Customer:

Promise #2:

ROCK & SAND

Profit Per X: Your Company's Unique KPI for Scaling Up

FOUR DECISIONS® Tools

Attributes of your Profit Per X:

- Single overarching KPI to scale your business
- Fundamental economic engine of your business
- Able to impact and optimize both revenue and cost of "X"
- Tightly aligns with your BHAG® (use same unit of measurement)

Fundamental Economic Engine (Scalable) = $\dfrac{\text{PROFIT}}{\text{X}}$

"Profit" This is an important financial unit that drives profit (e.g. gross profit, revenue, net profit)

"X" This is your fundamental building block for scaling the business, which you can act on to increase revenue and lower cost (e.g. airplanes, deliveries, clients)

Instructions:

- Each team member brainstorms individually
- Collaborate as a team to select two potential "profit" metrics and "X" building blocks
- Remember, your "X" should be consistent with your BHAG®

Profit KPI

Profit KPI

"X" Building Block

"X" Building Block

ROCK & SAND

The BHAG®: Your 10 to 30-Year North Star

FOUR DECISIONS® Tools

Big Hairy Audacious Goal (BHAG®) attributes:

- Arises from the Hedgehog overlap
- Challenges you to greatness
- Reinforces business fundamentals

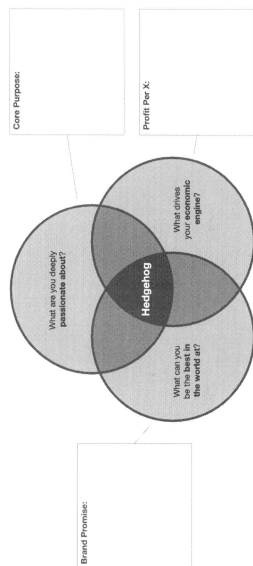

Core Purpose:

Profit Per X:

What are you deeply passionate about?

What drives your **economic engine?**

Hedgehog

What can you be the best in the world at?

Brand Promise:

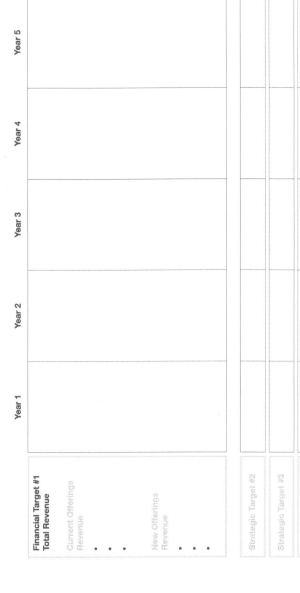

Strategic Targets: Aiming for Success

FOUR DECISIONS® Tools

	Year 1	Year 2	Year 3	Year 4	Year 5
Financial Target #1 **Total Revenue**					
Current Offerings Revenue • • •					
New Offerings Revenue • • •					
Strategic Target #2					
Strategic Target #3					
Strategic Target #4					
Strategic Target #5					

ROCK & SAND

Key Thrusts: Your 3 to 5-Year Chess Moves

FOUR DECISIONS® Tools

Review your 3-5 year targets:

- Revenue
- Gross margin
- BHAG®
- Profit Per X
- Labor productivity
- Team talent

Each team member:

- Develop 2 key thrusts (strategic actions over a 3-5 year time frame) that will position you to achieve your targets

Collaborate as a team:

- Rank the top 2 "chess moves" in each of the Four Decisions™
- Select and circle your top 5 key thrusts for the next 3-5 years

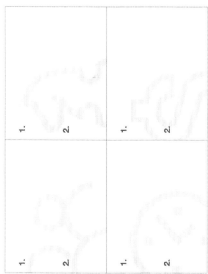

ROCK & SAND

Annual Initiatives: Top 5 and "First of Five"

FOUR DECISIONS® Tools

Instructions:

- As a team, identify and finalize your critical number(s)
- Individually, draft your company's top 5 priorities using your One-Page Strategic Plan as guidance
- As a team, debate and finalize the top 5 company priorities
- Using critical numbers as a guide, highlight your top priority "First of Five"
- Set personal accountability and completion date for each priority

Top 5 Priorities: Annual Initiatives

1.		LEADER
		DATE

2.		LEADER
		DATE

3.		LEADER
		DATE

4.		LEADER
		DATE

5.		LEADER
		DATE

ROCK & SAND

Quarterly Rocks: Top 3 to 5 Priorities

FOUR DECISIONS® Tools

Instructions:

- As a team, identify and finalize your critical number(s)
- Individually, draft your company's top 3 to 5 priorities using your One-Page Strategic Plan as guidance
- As a team, debate and finalize the top 3 to 5 company priorities
- Using critical numbers as a guide, highlight your top priority
- Set personal accountability and completion date for each priority

Top 3 to 5 Priorities: Quarterly Priorities

#	Priority	LEADER	DATE
1.			
2.			
3.			
4.			
5.			

ROCK & SAND

Meeting Rhythms: Setting the Organizational Heartbeat

FOUR DECISIONS® Tools

Communication Rhythm Action Plan:

- The top challenge in any organization is communication
- A series of 5 ongoing meetings will bring focus, alignment and save time
- Commit to a specific meeting schedule to establish communication rhythm

Individually:

- Suggest best times and dates for the 5 meeting rhythms

Date	Day of Week	Time
	DAILY HUDDLE	5 - 15 MINS
	WEEKLY MEETING	60 - 90 MINS
	MONTHLY MANAGEMENT MEETING	4 - 8 HOURS
	QUARTERLY PLANNING	1 - 2 DAYS
	ANNUAL PLANNING	1 - 3 DAYS

As a leadership team:

- Collaborate, choose, and calendar each meeting for the entire year

YEAR

	Time	Day	Date(s)
Daily Huddle			
Weekly Meeting			
Monthly Meeting			
Quarterly Planning			
Pre-Annual Planning			
Annual Planning			